de Marisco

de Marisco

A Family's Journey Through Time

Margaret Nyhon

Willow Press
Otago, New Zealand

Published by Willow Press, Otago, New Zealand

Contact author: margaretf@hotmail.co.nz

A catalogue record for this book is available from the National Library of New Zealand.

Contents

PART II. MODERN TIMES: THE MARRIS FAMILY

Acknowledgements

A special thank you to the following people.

Brent Marris of Marisco Vineyard, for his support in allowing me to use information on his family, vineyards and his speciality wine, The Kings Series. Thanks also for the use of the Lundy Island photos.

Christopher David Thompson, photographer of the wonderful Lundy Island photos.

Norman Crawshaw, for allowing me to use extracts from his book *Worlds Apart* which provides much of the material on the Lincolnshire Marris's and their West Coast descendants.

Guy Marris, John Marris, and Michael Marris, for their contributions.

Martin Taylor, who assisted me with publication of this book, for his time and patience. It must have been heavy going for him at times.

Maps

Map 1. Map of England showing locations of de Marisco lands and castles

Map 2. Map of Ireland showing locations of de Marisco lands and castles

Family trees

de Marisco origins: *Theory 1*

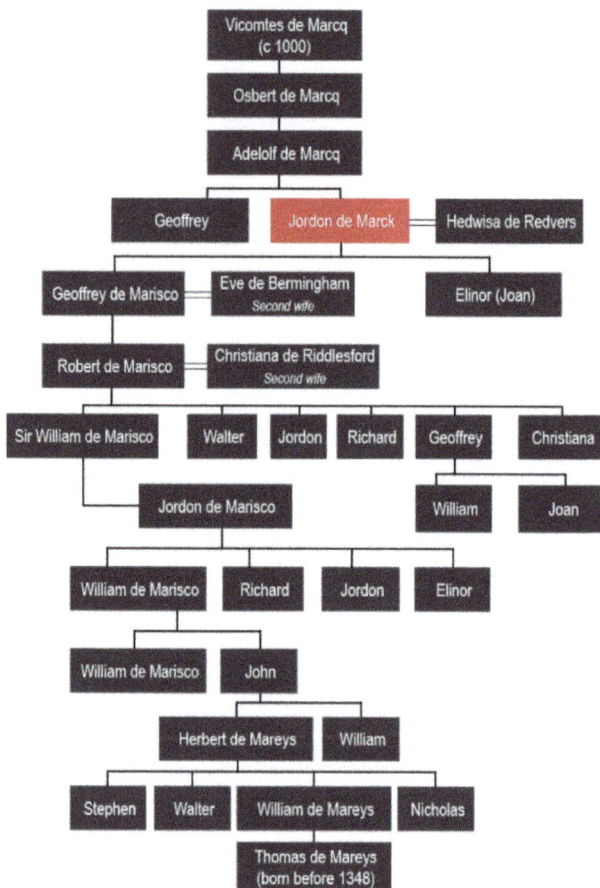

```
                    Vicomtes de Marcq
                        (c 1000)
                           |
                     Osbert de Marcq
                           |
                     Adelolf de Marcq
                           |
        ┌──────────────────┼──────────────────┐
     Geoffrey      Jordon de Marck ═══ Hedwisa de Redvers
                           |
        ┌──────────────────┴──────────┐
 Geoffrey de Marisco ═══ Eve de Bermingham      Elinor (Joan)
                           Second wife
        |
 Robert de Marisco ═══ Christiana de Riddlesford
                           Second wife
        |
  ┌─────────┬────────┬────────┬──────────┬───────────┐
Sir William   Walter  Jordon  Richard  Geoffrey   Christiana
de Marisco                                  |
        |                            ┌───────┴──────┐
 Jordon de Marisco                 William        Joan
        |
  ┌──────────┬────────┬────────┐
William de    Richard  Jordon  Elinor
Marisco
        |
  ┌──────────┬────────┐
William de     John
Marisco
        |
  ┌──────────┬────────┐
Herbert de Mareys  William
        |
  ┌────────┬────────┬──────────────┬──────────┐
Stephen  Walter  William de Mareys  Nicholas
                       |
              Thomas de Mareys
              (born before 1348)
```

Illustration 1. Family tree showing the origins of the de Mariscos, *Theory 1*

de Marisco origins: *Theory 2*

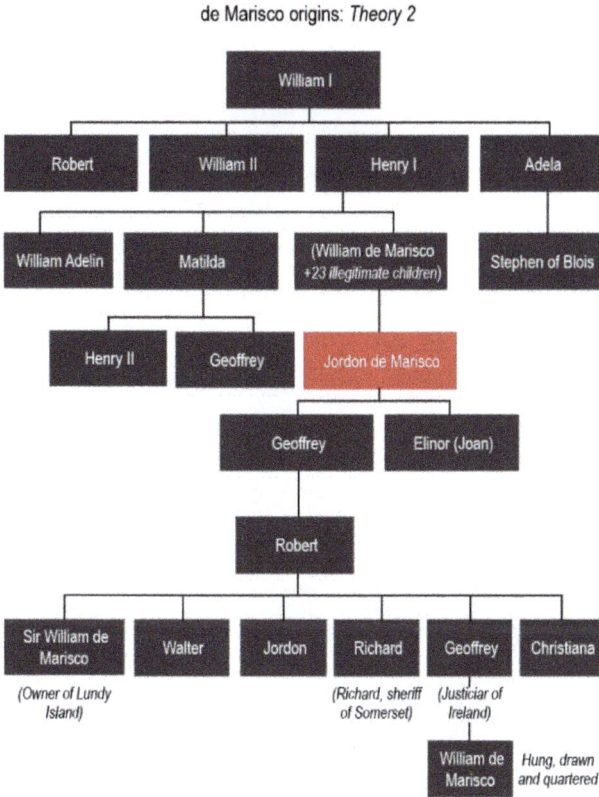

Illustration 2. Family tree showing the origins of the de Mariscos, *Theory 2*

Family trees

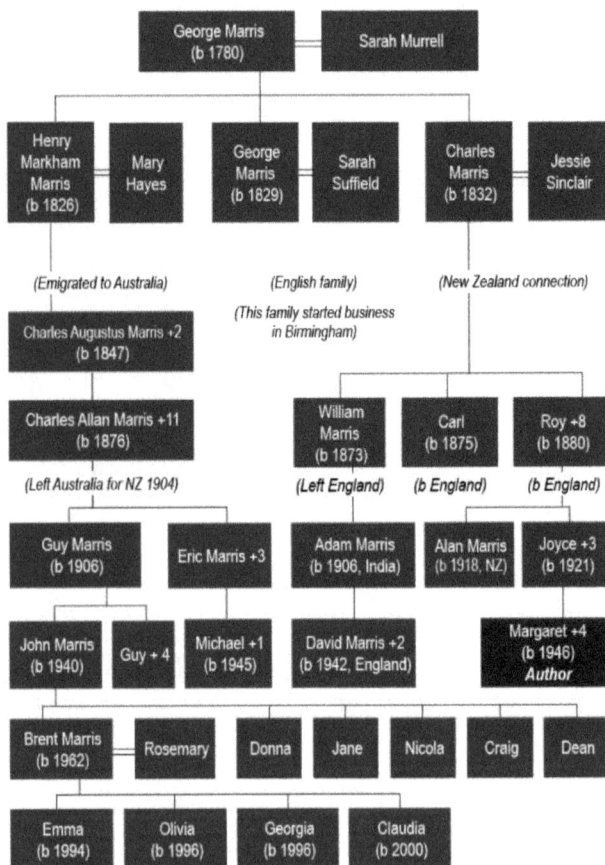

George Marris (b 1780) — Sarah Murrell

Henry Markham Marris (b 1826) — Mary Hayes

George Marris (b 1829) — Sarah Suffield

Charles Marris (b 1832) — Jessie Sinclair

(Emigrated to Australia)

(English family)
(This family started business in Birmingham)

(New Zealand connection)

Charles Augustus Marris +2 (b 1847)

Charles Allan Marris +11 (b 1876)

(Left Australia for NZ 1904)

William Marris (b 1873)

Carl (b 1875)

Roy +8 (b 1880)

(Left England)

(b England)

(b England)

Guy Marris (b 1906)

Eric Marris +3

Adam Marris (b 1906, India)

Alan Marris (b 1918, NZ)

Joyce +3 (b 1921)

John Marris (b 1940)

Guy + 4

Michael +1 (b 1945)

David Marris +2 (b 1942, England)

Margaret +4 (b 1946) *Author*

Brent Marris (b 1962)

Rosemary

Donna

Jane

Nicola

Craig

Dean

Emma (b 1994)

Olivia (b 1996)

Georgia (b 1996)

Claudia (b 2000)

Illustration 3. Family tree showing the modern era, Marris family

List of illustrations

Preface

My interest in family history sent me on a journey of discovery, full of surprises, shock, and total disbelief as to where our background began. Our ancestors' footprints left heavy dents in the lands of England, Ireland and Lundy Island. These footprints took me back in time to where their lives began and the wonderful history that accompanied this scandalous, but exciting, family.

I was totally unaware of my maternal grandfather's background. This turned out to be a real treasure trove of history that made me want to shout from the rooftops and let the world know what I had uncovered.

My ordinary family was ordinary no more!

Hence my story, connecting the past with the present, and awakening the history that accompanied this notorious family through the passage of time.

Introduction

The de Marisco family was from an Anglo-Norman background and maintained a tempestuous relationship with the English monarchy.

In my research on this family, I have come across many contradictory stories, which have been rather confusing at times. But my saviour was a journal kept by the Marris family in England, recording their history down through the generations. The writers of this journal were Reverend George Marris (born 1780), Harold Colquhoun Marris Esq. OBE (born 1883), and Tyrrell Marris (born 1930). This was their written record, kept for future Marris families.

The repeating of family names across generations has confused many historians who struggle to identify which generation certain members belonged to. Also, the de Marisco men in most instances had several wives, adding to the confusion.

While doing several years of research, I discovered that there was another side to the de Mariscos and where their lineage may have begun. Again, I have been met with conflicting stories. Did they come to England from Marcq in France, as recorded in the family journal? Or were they descendants of an illegitimate son of King Henry I, as some historians have recorded?

There is no actual evidence either way, only what has been recorded in books written by English historians. So now I am left in limbo, not knowing which of these versions is correct. I have elected to tell both sides of the story.

From this point the family saga continues with the building of a wealthy empire, acquiring strategic lands that earned them a place in English and Irish history. With the turning of the tides, fortunes and names changed throughout the following generations.

In Marlborough, New Zealand, the Marris family—descendants of the de Mariscos from Lundy Island—have developed a magnificent vineyard named Marisco Vineyards, honouring their family history.

The Kings Series is five wines: the King's Bastard Chardonnay, the King's Favour Sauvignon Blanc, the King's Thorn Pinot Gris, the King's Wrath Pinot Noir, and A Sticky End Noble Sauvignon Blanc.

These wines are marketed under the Marisco umbrella and are deserving of their names as they have been lovingly matched to the type of grapes suited to the concept of their own individual stories.

PART I

Origins of the de Mariscos

From the lineage and rich history of the de Mariscos evolved the Marris families, whose lives we will follow through to the present day. While many families remained in England, others spanned the globe. That indomitable spirit and determination that flowed through the blood of their de Marisco ancestors remained with them through all their adversities and throughout their journeys.

1

Who were the de Mariscos?

The de Mariscos were a highborn and influential family of Norman descent, with connections to France, England, Lundy Island, and Ireland. Along with this family came fame and shame, love and hatred, loyalty and treachery, and a solid place in English history. To understand their origins, we should first look into the origins of the Normans.

In AD 911 the Frankish King Charles (the Simple), in an effort to stop raids of his land, offered a large amount of land in Northern France to a band of Vikings, led by Rollo, in total obedience to the Frankish Crown. During the years of Duke Rollo's reign, the local term for 'Norsemen' slowly contracted to 'Norman'.

The Anglo-Normans were mainly the descendants of the Normans who ruled England following the Norman Conquest by William the Conqueror at the Battle of Hastings in 1066. A small number of Normans had earlier befriended future Anglo-Saxon King of England, Edward the Confessor, during his exile in his mother's homeland, Normandy. Edward was brought up in Normandy, and in 1042 brought masons to work on Westminster Abbey, the first Romanesque building in England.

In the year 1066, the Saxon-Dane rulers of England were overthrown and replaced by the new invaders—the Normans. Following the invasion, one of the things William I wanted to do was to establish Norman control. This was in part forced by the building of Motte and Bailey castles over the land (the Normans were well known for building castles) where the Norman Knights could have a base to subjugate the surrounding lands. The Normans were among the most travelled peoples of Europe.

Now that the Battle of Hastings was over, England submitted to its Norman overlords. The Normans seemed to combine up-to-date military skills and tactics with their own violent Scandinavian Viking Heritage. They had many vengeful Bretons backing them up.

Wherever the English arose against this usurpation of their rights and homeland, William the Conqueror would put the revolt down mercilessly and destructively. He left leaving the land uninhabitable, families homeless or butchered, villages wiped out, and towns ransacked and burned. Those left died of disease or hunger.

Also known as William the Bastard, he was the son of unmarried Robert and his mistress Herleva. When he became King of England, he wanted both England and the Duchy of Normandy. Only when the 'bastard's' English-born son, Henry, married Edith of Scotland, did the English begin accepting him. For it was through her that the ancient blood of the Royal House of Wessex had flowed, and only then would the descendants of William truly become heirs of the English throne which William had usurped and stolen.

On 25 December 1066, Archbishop Eldred placed the Crown of England on William the Bastard's head. William built castles everywhere and fortified pockets of land to defend against the enemy. This was the downfall of the English, as they were not prepared for invasion. In 1068 William marched on Exeter, which submitted, and he was given a castle. He continued his campaign in the North of England, Devon, Cornwell, Dorset and Somerset.

An Englishman looked towards the sky as if pleading for divine intervention, saying, "A cold Heart and a Bloody Hand, now rule the English Land."

In 1087 William the 'bastard' King was injured in a horse riding accident and suffered terrible pain, and died not long after. Orderic Vitalis (1075–1142, a Benedictine monk who wrote on Normandy and Anglo Norman England) recorded his dying words. "May god forgive me, for I have taken that which is not mine to take." So ended the life of William the Bastard, the usurper who sought to rule a land that was not his to rule, a land whose people he treated cruelly, a people he had no God-given right to persecute or govern.

He was followed by his son William Rufus II who was to be as cruel to the English people as his father.

2

Two theories of the de Marisco lineage

The task of putting together the de Marisco history was uncomplicated until I discovered that several English historians had named William de Marisco as an illegitimate son of King Henry I. A recent English author qualified this by writing that the de Marisco family coat of arms bore a lion rampant, the lion of England, though the coat of arms of the present Marris family does not support this.

On 7 January 1966 the English *Daily Telegraph* newspaper published a special article to mark the anniversary of the Norman Conquest. It named the Marris's as one of only four families who can prove that an ancestor fought for William of Normandy at the Battle of Hastings, nine centuries ago.

So I was left in limbo, not knowing which of these theories was correct. I've elected here to tell both sides of the story.

THEORY ONE: DE MARISCO LINEAGE FROM MARCQ IN FRANCE

We'll start with the most commonly-held theory of the origins of the de Mariscos. The Vicomte de Marcq came from a small town near Calais in France in about the year 1000. His younger son Osbert de Marcq held, under Walter Flandrensis in 1087, two hides in Horton (a hide is traditionally taken as 120 acres) and six hides in Evenlai (Evenly) Northamptonshire. Osbert married a lady of a Breton family. The Breton families were descendants of the Celtic tribes who were granted lands by King William for their assistance at the Battle of Hastings in 1066. They came to hold important positions in the Norman nobility of England, forging alliances through arranged marriages with the King of Scotland.

They had one known son, Adelolf de Marcq (de Merk). He was one of the twenty-seven known companions of William on the battlefield. For this he was awarded the Manors of Little Holland, Lincolnshire, and Tolleshunt and Leleford. According to the Doomsday Book (Essex), he held from Count Eustace II, Marks Hall (Figure 1) in Latton and Marks Manor in Dunmow. In Cambridgeshire he held one hide at Croxton from Hardwin de Scalers (Hardouin d'Escaliers), a Norman noble who had come from France with William the Conqueror as a steward of his household. He received a number of domains in Hertfordshire and Cambridgeshire from a grateful William.

Figure 1. Marks Hall mansion, Essex

Ultimately, Adelolf succeeded to his father's lands in Northamptonshire. He married a daughter of William de la Launde de Patry. (The women were often referred to as sister of, or daughter of.) They had two known sons, Geoffrey and Jordon. Geoffrey de Marcq is mentioned in the Essex Pipe Rolls of 1129–1130 and held land in Herefordshire. He married and had a family, but later returned to Marcq in France and became a Monk at Maule, near Calais.

Jordon de Marcq served at Mont St Michel, Brittany, with Prince Henry and Baldwin de Redvers. The Island of Mont St Michel is located approximately one kilometre from the

Normandy coast and was only accessible at low tide. The King of Franks agreed to grant the island to the Bretons in the year 867. In 1067 the Monastery of Mont St Michel gave its support to Duke William of Normandy in his claim to the throne of England.

When Henry became King, Jordon de Marcq (later also known as Jordon de Marisco) received from him Cumberton in Cambridgeshire and the farm of Clipston in Nottinghamshire. Jordon married Hedwisa, daughter of Baldwin de Redvers. Baldwin de Redvers was made Earl of Devon by Empress Matilda after she established herself in England in early 1141. He founded several monasteries, notably those of Quarr Abbey in the Isle of Wight, and the Priory of St James at Exeter.

THEORY TWO: WAS JORDON DE MARCQ DESCENDED FROM KING HENRY I?

Before we continue the de Marisco story, let's digress briefly to consider an alternative theory: Was Jordon de Marcq—a key figure in the de Marisco family lineage—in fact descended from King Henry I via one of his numerous illegitimate sons, William de Marisco?

William I, son of William the Conqueror, married Queen Matilda of Flanders who was the daughter of Baldwin V de Lille, count of Flanders, and Adele Capet, princess of France. They had four sons and three daughters. William I split his kingdom between his two eldest sons, William and Robert. Another son, Richard, died young.

William Rufus II was given England and reigned from 1057–1100. Robert was given Normandy and became the Duke of Normandy. No land was given to Henry Beauclere because as the youngest son he was expected to become a Bishop. When William Rufus II was shot dead while out with a shooting party—which his brother Henry was part of—Henry rushed home and seized the throne. Was this a planned ploy for Henry to take the throne? Henry Beauclere became King Henry I in 1100.

His brother Robert managed Normandy badly and the Normans wanted him gone, so they invited King Henry I to take the Dukedom of Normandy. Henry led an English army into Normandy, which he took from his feckless brother at The Battle of Tinchebray. Robert was taken prisoner by his brother and imprisoned in Cardiff Castle, Wales, where he lived for 28 years until his death.

Henry I further cemented his popularity by marrying Edith of Scotland, the daughter of Malcolm Canmore (Malcolm Greathead), King of the Scots, and the Saxon, St Margaret (sister of Edgar Atheling) of the Saxon Royal House. Edith—or Matilda as she became—was a good and much-respected Queen. Although Henry was seldom faithful to his Queen, theirs was considered a good marriage by royal standards.

King Henry I was the King, "who would let no one break the law—but himself". He was shrewd, tough, ambitious and brutal. His name, Beauclerc, denoted his good education and he was probably the first Norman King to be fluent in English.

Henry I claimed England, promising to govern according to the old laws of England. He carried out social and judicial reforms which included issuing the Charter of Liberties, and restoring the English laws of King Edward the Confessor.

In November 1120, King Henry triumphed by getting the French King Louis XI to agree to securing the long-disputed lands of the Grand Duchy of Normandy. These were to pass into the hands of King Henry's son, William Adelin, upon Henry's death. It was to culminate in one of the worst shipping disasters in England's royal history.

King Henry I arranged as a political alliance the marriage of his son William (aged between 12 and 15 years) to Isobella d'Anjou who was 12 years old, daughter of Count Fulk V of Anjou. The young William was taken to Anjou to marry. Then, leaving his bride behind, he returned to England with his father.

Just as the King was about to embark on his homeward journey, a man named Thomas FitzStephen approached him and said, "I have a vessel which is aptly called the *White Ship* excellently fitted out, and ready for the Royal Service". He added that his grandfather, Airard, had served King Henry's father, William I in carrying the Norman Duke across the Channel when he invaded England. Henry replied, "Your request meets my approval, but I have indeed chosen a fine ship for myself and will not change it, but I will entrust to you, my son William Adelin, and many nobles of my Realm".

Among those who got on the ship were two of King Henry's illegitimate children, Richard and Matilda. One report suggests there were close to three hundred people on board, including fifty crew who manned the oars. According to the chronicler, 'Orderic Vitalis' wine was being handed out freely, and passengers and crew alike were indulging themselves. A few people decided to get off the ship because of the state of the crew. This included Stephen of Blois, the King's nephew, who complained of having diarrhoea.

At length, the *White Ship* (*la Blanche Nef*) left the shores and put to sea. The drunken oarsmen rowed with all their might, encouraged by the merry crowd aboard. But the guard on lookout did not notice the rocks to the port side of the vessel. It struck the rocks violently and the ship capsized without warning, throwing everyone into the water. Cries were heard from the land but, because it was too dark, there was little anyone could do. All aboard the ship perished, apart from one survivor, a butcher from Rouen named Berold.

There was much debate about this disaster, whether it was a ploy by several parties to serve their own end. One was Stephen of Blois who, upon King Henry's death, became King of England.

King Henry I was devastated as not only had he lost his only legitimate son, but also the future heir to the throne of

England. It was said he never smiled again. He then took a second wife, the beautiful young Adelicia, daughter of Geoffrey VII, Count of Louvain. Adelicia bore Henry no children before he died. She did however go on to have many children to her second husband.

The King then turned to his daughter, Matilda, who at the age of eleven had been betrothed by her father, in a political alliance to the 32-year-old German, Henry V, the Holy Roman Emperor. This was not a very long marriage as the Holy Roman Emperor died young. Matilda, now known as the 'Empress,' was summoned back to England from Germany by her father.

The proud and haughty Matilda, aged about 25, was ordered reluctantly into an arranged marriage to 15-year-old Geoffrey Plantagent, her brother-in-law and the son of Count d'Anjou. William Adelin had married Fulk's daughter, but the *White Ship* disaster put an end to this, thus not cementing an alliance between Henry and Anjou. King Henry's preference was to use Matilda's marriage to secure the southern borders of Normandy by marrying her to Geoffrey. Matilda personally loathed this man, as he did her. King Henry, who was desperate for an heir to the throne, ordered the pair to do their duty leading to the birth of the future King, Henry II, and his younger brother Geoffrey.

King Henry I died aged 67, his death caused by eating too much of the fish called Lamprey, against his doctor's orders. He was buried at Reading Abbey. The Abbey was destroyed during the Reformation and no trace of Henry's tomb survived. Nearby, a small plaque and a large memorial cross have been erected in the adjourning Forbury Gardens.

King Henry I proved to be a serial adulterer and begat more illegitimate children than any other English King. During his reign, he had fathered twenty-four—perhaps more—children by a continuous string of mistresses. None of these children could become royal subjects, but one of these illegitimate sons, called William, is thought to be the beginning of the de Marisco line.

William Adelin's death led to a succession crisis and a period of civil war in England known as the Anarchy. Matilda, as the late King's daughter, was to succeed him to the throne. But the barons, who had vowed to support the accession of Empress Matilda to the throne, reneged, and Matilda's cousin, Stephen of Blois, seized the throne to become King of England.

Stephen ruled for approximately four years, until Matilda and her husband Geoffrey of Anjou, the founder of the Plantagenet dynasty and a traditional enemy of England's Norman nobles, launched a devastating war against King Stephen and his allies. This was for the control of the English throne. The Anarchy continued from 1135–1153.

In 1153, a compromise was reached in the Treaty of Wellingford. By its terms, King Stephen was to retain the crown for the remainder of his lifetime, whereupon it would revert to Matilda's son, Henry II, and his heirs. King Stephen died the following year and was succeeded by Henry II who became the first of the great Plantagenet dynasty.

Several English historians claim that William de Marisco was one of King Henry I's illegitimate sons. The de Marisco family coat of arms bares a lion rampant, the head of England, signifying perhaps that they may well have been entitled to royal rights—although those of the present English descendants do not support this.

3

Early history of the de Marisco family

As this alternative theory shows, there is some doubt about the lineage of the key figure of Jordon de Marcq in the Marisco family history. But let's now return to him and to what we know of his descendants.

In the period prior to 1155, de Marcq married Hedwise de Redvers and they had two children, a son Geoffrey and a daughter Elinor (Joan). Elinor married John FitzThomas of Devon. The FitzThomas family owned land in Shanid, Limerick, Ireland.

Geoffrey de Marisco—the name had now changed—held half a Knight's fee in Huntspill, Somerset and the Honour of Brampton, Devon. A Knight's fee was a measure of land that was deemed sufficient for a Knight and his squires to be equipped with horses and armour to fight for their overlord when needed. Geoffrey was also mentioned in the Essex Pipe Roll of 1130–31, a collection of financial records maintained by the English Treasury.

There are conflicting stories on who Geoffrey married. One record lists his first wife as Jane Esserby, his second wife as Eve de Bermingham, and a third wife as Alice, sister of Hugh de Lacy. Another only lists two wives. This again is confusing. There were two known children, Joan de Marisco who married Theobald FitzWalter Le Boteler, and a son, Robert de Marisco.

Eve de Bermingham, one of Geoffrey's wives, was an heiress of Offaly. Eve was a Norman Irish heiress and the only child of Robert de Bermingham. The de Bermingham family held the Lordship of Birmingham in England for 400 years, and turned it from a small village into a thriving market town. They also helped to invade Ireland and were rewarded with the Barony of Athenry. Robert de Bermingham was enfeoffed by Strongbow with part of the Kingdom of Ui Failghe, a Gaelic-Irish Kingdom which existed up to the year 1550 but is now known as County Offaly. Eve had been married twice before, first to Gerald FitzMaurice, and upon his death she inherited all his Irish lands; and secondly to Geoffrey FitzRobert. Eve's third marriage was to Geoffrey de Marisco. The lands in Offaly were her inheritance, and they went with her to Geoffrey who was entitled to hold them for his life, even after Eve died. The de Marisco fortune was steadily growing.

Their son, Robert de Marisco, was tenant-in-Chief of Devon and held six Knight's fee in Lincolnshire. He is mentioned in the Devon Pipe Roll of 1175–1180. Robert first married a sister of John Comyn, the Archbishop of Dublin, and they had five sons: William, Walter, Jordon, Richard, and Geoffrey. Robert de Marisco's second marriage was to Christiana de Riddlesford, and they had a daughter Christiana, named after her mother.

Robert's eldest son, William de Marisco, was of Huntspill and Cameley in Somerset. He was the first de Marisco to occupy Lundy Island. It is not known if it was owned or only occupied by the de Mariscos. This will be referred to later. Sir William, as he was known, married Lucy, daughter of Alexander d'Alneto, Lord of Cameley in Somerset. In about 1150 the Manor of Cameley was given to Bath Abbey by the d'Alneto family. In the thirteenth century it was held by the de Marisco family until it passed into the control of the Knights Templar, which was confirmed in a grant of 1201. During the late thirteenth and early fourteenth centuries, the manor was again under the control of the de Mariscos. This ambitious family never gave up any of their land without a fight.

One historian, Gerry Brooke, writing in the *Bristol Post* (9 March 2010), said of the de Mariscos: "They were a shifty family … who were later declared outlaws".

In 1197, another of Robert's sons, Richard de Marisco, appears as one of the officers of the Exchequer and a rising cleric. He was a prebend at Exeter in 1209, then a rector in Oxfordshire, Archdeacon of Northumberland by 1212, and in that year also became sheriff of Dorset and Somerset. From a vicarage in Worcestershire, he was entrusted to gather the ecclesiastical takings. He was essentially one of King John's favourites and an influential courtier. He negotiated for the King when he quarrelled with the Pope, and became Chancellor of the Realm circa 1214. Richard continued in office after the King's death. He seemed to have been outstanding, even among the de Mariscos, for his disreputable character.

In 1217, after King John's death, he was made Bishop of Durham on the recommendation of the Pope. Richard de Marisco died in 1226 on his way to London to plead his case in a dispute with the Monks. The dispute with the Monks was so costly that it long burdened the Bishopric of Durham, and it was said that, "Richard was Bishop for fifteen years after his death."

Jordon de Marisco was sire and baron de Marisco, lord of Cameley, and Huntspill, and third son of Robert, whom he followed in the office of Lord Chamberlain to the King. He obtained from his brother Geoffrey, the baron of Kells, the Manor of Kilry, which he gave to the church, and the tithes to the priory of Lesnes in Kent.

GEOFFREY DE MARISCO

Geoffrey, Robert de Marisco's youngest son, was an important political figure in his time. Geoffrey was Lord of Thorney and Huntspill in Somerset. He was also the nephew of the Archbishop of Dublin, Ireland, and related to King Henry II. He received large grants of land in Ireland from King John who reigned from 1199.

In 1208 Geoffrey assumed the dignity of an ancient Irish dynasty. He was in his day the greatest and most powerful Lord of the name Montmorency, in either France or England.

Geoffrey de Marisco was Justiciar (chief governor) of Ireland for eight years between 1215 and 1223. He was thus well placed to grab a good bit of Leinster and Munster for himself. He tried to confiscate Terryglass in County Tipperary on the flimsy excuse that the Norman owner had not fortified it strongly enough, having built a stone house instead of a castle. The Normans were big on fortified castles.

The fact that a child King, Henry III, was on the throne did not exactly give Geoffrey a free hand in managing the affairs of Ireland, but he took it anyway. One of his tricks was to keep the taxes he collected in the King's name, and to spend the money, thus building many castles. As one chronicler put it tactfully, "more at his own free will, than according to the King's commands". Geoffrey resigned as Justiciar of Ireland on the King's request, because of financial irregularities. He had not paid the revenue of the crown to the Exchequer in Dublin. When this was all settled, he was reappointed as Justiciar from 1226–1228.

Most of his exploits were bloody and power-driven. He was content to take land from the native and fellow Normans alike. His ruthless and treacherous pursuits meant he held sway in places as far apart as Blessington, County Wicklow, and Castleisland in County Kerry.

Adare Castle, Limerick, Ireland (Figure 2) —also known as Desmond Castle—is an Anglo-Norman castle beside the river Maigue, and was built just before 1200. The first mentioned owner was Geoffrey de Marisco, who had a few castles around Ireland. It changed hands a number of times during its lifetime, and is linked to some interesting history. Adare Abbey was the only Trinitarian establishment in Ireland and had been invited there by Geoffrey de Marisco.

Figure 2. Adare Castle, Limerick, Ireland

Geoffrey was described as, "a second wave archetypical Anglo-Norman robber baron". He visited Palestine as a soldier and is the founder of the Knights Hospitallers of St John of Jerusalem who today are the Knights of Malta. In addition to the Trinitarian Abbey, Geoffrey also invited the Knights Hospitaller to establish a commandery, in 1215, in nearby Aney (now Hospital). The motive for Norman Barons to settle military and religious orders on their properties was not entirely pious, but it guaranteed that associated (and tithe-paying) lands would be safe and their values increased.

A very early record for the de Marisco family can be found at the Abbey in Hospital, County Limerick. A plaque on the gate reads: "Hospital Church, Founded by Geoffrey de Marisco as a Commander of Knights Hospitallers. Inside the building are three effigies, one of a double tomb of a Knight and his Lady, another believed to cover the tomb of the founder." This plaque is still there today.

Geoffrey de Marisco owned many Irish castles. Rindoon castle was one of the most important Norman Castles in Connacht. Some form of fortification was already present at Rindoon. In 1227, Geoffrey chose this as the site of the new Norman settlement. Rindoon Castle was situated on the north side of the peninsula in Lough Ree, surrounded by water but for the north side. Rinn Duin (Rindoon) became a place of strategic importance in the thirteenth and fourteenth centuries. Whoever controlled Rindoon Castle controlled

Lough Ree. The ruins of these castles can be seen today. (Figure 3)

Figure 3. Rindoon Castle ruins. *Photographed by Gerry Dwyer*
www.irelandswildlandscapes.com

Castleisland castle in Kerry was built by Geoffrey in 1220. It formed a line of Norman castles along the river Maine as a defence between the Normans of North Kerry and the native Irish of South Kerry. It was a massive structure, stretching northward from the bank of the river Maine to the foot of Maum Hill, a distance of well over one mile, and the same distance to the East. The only part of the ruin remaining today is the Marisco Tower, which is located behind the terrace of houses on the Killarney Road. (Figure 4)

Geoffrey fell into temporary disgrace with the King, in a conspiracy against the Earl Marshall. He was implicated in the death of Richard Marshall at the Battle of the Curragh in Ireland in 1234, and many thought he had betrayed Marshall who at the time was fighting partisans of Henry III. Geoffrey and his son William were briefly imprisoned after Marshall's death. Brendan Smith in *Britain and Ireland, 900–1300* thinks it was because they were scapegoated by King Henry who had plenty of reasons for wanting Marshall eliminated, but could not openly admit it because of his popularity.

Figure 4. Castleisland ruins Kerry, Ireland

Geoffrey de Marisco was not above treason, and accusations were brought against him and his son William. Geoffrey had to flee the country and died in poverty in France in 1245. His body was brought back to Ireland and he was buried in the tomb at Hospital Church (Figure 5). His son William, along with his father, was accused of the murder of a clerk, Henry Clement, and of a plot against the King, but this was not proven. William fled to safety on Lundy Island which belonged to his uncle, Sir William de Marisco.

The thirteenth century historian Mathew Paris (1200–1259), a Benedictine monk and English chronicler, said unlovingly of Geoffrey in Vol III of *Chronica Majora* (1250):

> About this time, Geoffrey Marsh (de Marisco), a man who had been formerly noble, and not the least one amongst the magnates of Ireland, and who had incurred an indelible stain by the treacherous murder of Earl Richard Marshall, and who now was an exile ... having been expelled from Scotland, banished from England and disinherited in Ireland, after the ignominious death of his son [William, whom we will mention later] and the loss of all his friends, was himself taken from amongst us; thus finally ending so many deaths of his own.

Geoffrey's line of male descendants died out in the fourteenth century, and so fell a rotten, though colourful, branch from the de Marisco tree.

Geoffrey de Marisco had taken part in many Norman attacks on the Irish in Connacht. This was to leave a legacy since the Morris family, one of the famous tribes of Galway, owe their descent to him.

Over the past 800 years, the de Mariscos multiplied and their Irish descendants are likely to be today's Morrissays, who originated from that part of Ireland.

Figure 5. Tomb of Geoffrey de Marisco at Hospital Church, Ireland

CHRISTIANA DE MARISCO

Robert de Marisco's second wife Christiana de Riddlesford was the daughter and heiress of Walter de Riddlesford and Annora de Riddlesford (born Plantagenet). Walter was born in Kildare in Ireland, and Annora came from Salisbury, Wiltshire in England.

Walter de Riddlesford (Baron of Leinster) had lands granted to him in 1238 as an underlord. He built a castle on his land, and a few years later both Walter and his wife died, thus leaving two infant daughters, Christiana and Emmeline. The Crown took custody of their possessions, and ordered an inquiry into their properties. Later, Christiana married Robert de Marisco and Emmeline married Hugh de Lacy, Earl of Ulster. Robert and Christiana had one child, a daughter called Christiana, who upon her mother's death became heiress to half of the de Riddlesford fortune. There were the manors of Tristtledermot and Kilkea in Leinster (Figure 6) as well as tenant of the Crown Lands at Bray and the Vale of Dublin.

Figure 6. Kilkea Castle in Leinster, Ireland

Walter de Riddlesford's other lands included the Northern part of the Baron of Clare in Galway, and the manors of Headford and Corofin in Ireland.

Christiana's father, Robert de Marisco, died in Lucca while returning from a pilgrimage to Palestine. His epitaph is in Bath Abbey. Christiana, born in 1234, was still a minor when her father died. She had no control over her marital fate as that was in the hands of the King—all heiresses became wards of the King.

In Anglo-Norman society, heiresses acted as conduits who might bring to their husbands title lands and sometimes even family names. Christiana de Marisco, her aunty Emmeline de Riddlesford and Matilda de Lacy were three wealthy heiresses. They were an especially important element in Anglo-Norman Ireland. In a society concerned with the strengthening of kinship and alliances, marriage was in the minds of many men. Heiresses were the embodiment of vast potential in the newly conquered Irish territory. The king generally took great interest in the rights of wardship and marriage over heiresses, and often this disrupted or cemented the marital arrangements of his landholders.

Christiana became lady-in-waiting in the household of Eleanor of Provence, queen consort of King Henry III of England. In medieval society, the rights of vulnerable women to inherit the lands of their ancestors was enshrined and protected. Heiresses were a common occurrence in the families of the invaders and settlers of Ireland, and they enjoyed their legal rights.

The tide of support for heiresses began to ebb in the latter stages of the thirteenth century, although Anglo-Norman Ireland produced a large number of substantial heiresses who acted as the entry point for various men to Ireland. A classic case of this was the Genevre brothers, whose marriage to Christiana de Marisco and Matilda de Lacy was sanctioned by the King. The barons who held land in Ireland were upset with their King, as their ideas certainly didn't involve the two Savoyard brothers to whom the heiresses were awarded. Ebulo was a household knight of Henry III and was from the family of Humbert, Count of Geneva.

Ebulo de Genevre was granted both custody of Christiana's lands and her marriage by the King in 1246. She would have been of an age to marry by then—about fourteen years old. Ebulo and Christiana's marriage was short lived, (he must have died young) and she was without heirs for the rest of her life. She remained unmarried and enjoyed great favour with the King and Queen. She looked after her inheritance remarkably well. That Christiana was a favoured subject of the King and Queen and their family was beyond doubt. Christiana chose to stay single and not to be at the mercy of sometimes-unscrupulous guardians who used them as pawns in the plans of the King and his advisors. That she was allowed to remain unmarried shows that she was undoubtedly a royal favourite.

Because her lands were scattered all over Ireland and she had officers that administered her lands in her absence, this was cause for her to be cheated. In 1280 Christiana decided to get rid of her lands in Ireland. King Edward I agreed to do a swap with her.

The deal she agreed to was as follows:

> Render to the King and Queen all her castles, fortresses, lands with advowsons of churches, knight's fees, homage and services, villains and their offspring etc. in Ireland, on condition that the lands shall be extended and the King and Queen, when they have seisin thereof, shall give to her, lands in England to the same value, for life and three years after her death so that she may make her will, and assign the goods and profits of the land to whom may inherit.

Therefore, her half of the de Marisco and the de Riddlesford lands in Ireland, built up since the twelfth century, were in the firm grip of the King. After Queen Eleanor died in 1290, Christiana received back some of her Irish lands. They were still in the King's hands, but as she had leased them to the Queen for the term of her life, the King ordered them to be returned to her.

Christiana's influence in Ireland had waned, but never disappeared, and in 1293 she suddenly received all her Irish lands back. Thus upon her death with no heirs, the fortunes, lands and castles of those wealthy families that Christiana had inherited, went to the King. They were lost forever from the de Marisco and de Riddlesford families.

4

Lundy Island

This rugged island, lying just off the coast of Devon, offers a microcosm of British history within its barely two square mile area. If there were ever to be an island that would qualify as a Treasure Island by circumstances, then this would be that island. (Figure 7)

Figure 7. Lundy Island. *Photographed by Christopher D. Thompson*

The Normans came to Devon in 1068. The eldest son of King Harold led 64 ships from Ireland to the mouth of the Taw, where the Normans defeated them. Early records show that the Norman family de Newmarch held the Island circa 1140. The first mention of the de Marisco family occurred circa 1154.

Some records state that Lundy Island was leased to the de Mariscos while other records contradict this, saying that it was owned by the Knights Templar. Originally a great Norman family, the de Mariscos had spread throughout Europe. They were the first tyrannical Lundy Island owners (or occupiers) of which anything is known. In the twelfth century they became—as was the habit of Knights with Norman blood in their veins—very ambitious and powerful. They recognised in the Island a stronghold that could be held against all-comers—and hold it they did.

DE MARISCO FAMILY OCCUPATION

The de Marisco families, from their stronghold on the Island, maintained a tempestuous relationship with the English monarchy, at times receiving royal favour—was this because William was, in fact, the illegitimate son of King Henry I?—and yet ultimately, for the activities of piracy and treason, incurring the full and tragic vehemence of the King's displeasure.

The first mention of Lundy was to Sir William de Marisco, described in *Burke* as William de Marisco of Huntspill and Cameley, Somerset, and of Lundy Island. According to the

Encyclopaedia Brittanica, the elder William had built a castle on Lundy (Figure 8). In 1155 King Henry II, anxious to prevent attack from the French, was keen to take possession of the English Islands. This included the Isle of Lundy which he had granted to the Knights Templar. The de Mariscos refused to comply and remained in possession of the Island. From that time onwards, they caused all manner of problems for the English Kings.

Figure 8. Marisco Castle, Lundy Island

In July 1189, King Richard the Lionheart confirmed the grant of Lundy to the Templar. However William de Marisco refused to hand it over, an act for which he was fined 200 marks and outlawed. By 1197, however, he was back in favour. Later he was found to be fighting for the King of France.

By 1200, King John confirmed that Lundy belonged to the

Templar, but they had to pay 1000 pounds for this privilege. William de Marisco pledged his manor at Huntspill to guarantee his gift of Lundy to the Templar, but the Island was still not handed over. By this time William and his supporters were plying a trade in piracy from Lundy and, strangely enough, neither the King nor the Templar seemed able or even willing to do anything about this situation.

By 1202, during the reign of King John, Lundy was cut off from essential supplies because the Sheriff of Devon was forced to defend his ports against Sir William de Marisco. William was by now regularly using Lundy as a base to attack ships and traders along the North Devon Coast. In 1204 the King granted William the Manor of Braunton, and appointed him as head of some of his galleys. Perhaps this was a sweetener, to try and encourage loyalty, not rebellion. This clearly did not work.

By 1217, William had sided with many of his English barons in supporting Louis of France against King John. At the Battle of Sandwich, William was captured and put in prison for his part in the battle.

The following year Henry III had acceded to the throne. Peace was negotiated and all the prisoners were set free, including William. Surprisingly, he was given back his Island of Lundy and even allowed to move his mangonels from his lands at Cameley to Lundy. Mangonels were medieval artillery—stone throwing machines that were very destructive. This was the era before gunpowder.

In 1220, the Templar were given 100 shillings recompense for the loss of Lundy, as it was omitted from the charter dated 1227 by King Henry III that indicated its return to the de Mariscos. Three years later William de Marisco died peacefully in his sleep and was succeeded by his son Jordon.

Lundy was a royal rabbit warren, as rabbit skins were highly sought after, making a good income for the Island, and often used for the payment of work done there. Sir William de Marisco's nephew, William, installed himself as a fugitive on Lundy and for seven years had a right royal time. He collected around him as pretty a company of outlaws and malefactors as can be imagined. He fortified the Island and built a stronghold at the only landing place in the ten-mile coastline.

He led a piratical life, and with his men became pirates on the Irish Sea. They concentrated their depredations on shipping to Dublin and Drogheda, which prompted Dublin to beef up its city walls. They also plundered vessels which navigated the Bristol Channel, taking from them wine and provisions, and made predatory invasions on the Devonshire coast. Ships were forced to navigate close to Lundy Island because of the dangerous shingle banks in the fast-flowing River Severn and the Bristol Channel. Its tide range of 27ft (8.2m) is one of the greatest in the world.

Because the ships had to sail close to Lundy to negotiate the channel, many were shipwrecked in the wild seas. As well, this made the island a profitable location from which to prey on passing Bristol-bound merchant ships bringing valuable goods back from overseas. Some 'victims' from ships would be taken back for ransom, others as slaves, and those that proved obstinate were simply thrown over the cliffs to their deaths. (Figure 9)

Figure 9. The rugged coastline of Lundy Island. *Photographed by Christopher D. Thompson*

While William was at sea, the King seized his wife Matilda, his four sons, and two daughters. Matilda owned castles at Coonagh and Blathach near Limerick in Ireland. This was her generous marriage portion, given by her Uncle Henry, Archbishop of Dublin. These were also seized.

In 1142, and already under royal 'watch' for piracy off the coast of England, one William de Marisco was implicated in an assassination attempt on King Henry III. Found guilty of high treason, William, along with sixteen of his associates, were all sentenced to death.

The King was so displeased with William that he requested a special punishment—that of 'quartering'. He was dragged by his feet through the streets from Westminster to the Tower of London, to the penal machine vulgarly known as the gibbet where he was hung, drawn and quartered. Following his execution, his body was disembowelled, and four parts of William de Marisco's body were sent to the four corners of the Kingdom as an example of what would happen to those incurring the full vehemence of the King's wrath.

A Marisco descendant from Canada who visited the Tower of London was shown by a yeoman William de Marisco's name in the registry, as having been hung, drawn and quartered.

The de Mariscos held Lundy Island on and off for 200 years.

WHO WERE THE KNIGHTS TEMPLAR?

In the beginning, the overall commander of the Order of the Knights Templar was the Pope, and the Templar owed allegiance only to him. The first Grand Master of the Order was French nobleman Hugh de Payens from Champagne in France, who came to the British Isles in 1128 looking for support of the newly founded Order.

In that year, Hugh of the Knights Templar came to King Henry I in Normandy and was received with great ceremony. The King sent him to England where he was welcomed by all good men. He was given treasure by all in England and Scotland, including gold and silver, which was sent to Jerusalem. As a result, many people travelled to Jerusalem. This was to attract Knights to the new Order, to collect funds, and to establish the Order of the British Isles. Donations of land were given immediately. In Scotland, King David I was impressed by the virtues of this new Order of Knights, and his wife Matilda gave them land.

In 1200 King John reaffirmed an earlier gift to the order of Cameley and Temple Cloud. The Templar held mills and manors in Somerset, and were involved in sheep farming at Temple Hydon.

The Knights Templar were granted special status by the English Kings which exempted them from export and import duties and tax at all bridges and highways. As the Templar spread across England acquiring further lands and manors, they emerged as feudal overlords who managed their lands meticulously, thus allowing them to raise large amounts of revenue to support the Crusades in the Holy Land. The Templar labourers, servants, craftsmen etc. would have a Templar cross on their dwelling doors, denoting that they were exempt from tithes, and showing they were Templar subjects.

They always had a good relationship with the Kings of England and were considered honest and trustworthy. They had to take the monastic vows of poverty and owned nothing themselves. Everything belonged to the Order.

The Templar also established the first banking system in Europe, which meant the medieval traveller or pilgrim could deposit money with the Knights at one preceptor, and withdraw it at another, thus enabling them to travel freely, without fear of being robbed. Sadly, despite being very successful in businesses such as banking and shipping enterprises, once the Holy Land was lost, the situation changed drastically for the Knights Templar.

In 1307 King Philip IV of France stated that every Templar in France was to be arrested. He was envious of their wealth and power, and he owed them a great deal of money. Ultimately, many were cruelly burnt at the stake. The English Templar did not suffer until 1308, when King Edward II finally called for their capture. He didn't act as harshly as King Philip. After the suppression of the Templar in 1312, the majority of their possessions passed to the Hospitallers.

5

Jordon de Marisco and his descendants

Sir William de Marisco's son, Jordon, like his father, was of Huntspill and Cameley in Somerset, of Lundy Island and also of Corkeduffeney in Ireland.

The surname 'de Marisco' does not have native connotations and initially was not a name one would associate with Cloughjordon. However, when the origins of the Morris, Morrissey or Fitzmaurice clans—all three being derivatives of the name de Marisco—are explored, it would seem that the de Marisco name has a close and inextricable link with the very founding of the town Cloughjordon itself. Cloughjordon began as an inhabited settlement during the Norman lordship of Ireland in the thirteenth and fourteenth centuries. The de Marisco family was allocated land in Ormand, under the overlordship of the Butlers, by King Henry II. One unit of the de Mariscos moved into this area, took over the territory and built a stone castle and manor house, guarded by a moat surrounding the dwelling.

Jordon de Marisco became Seignior of Latteragh and Nenagh, and may have been the founder of the settlement which became known as Cloughjordon. Jordon visited the Holy Land and, on his return to Ireland, brought with him a stone which he inserted into the foundations of his tower house. Centuries later, this became the basis of the house now known as Cloughjordon House.

The stone, brought back from the banks of the River Jordon, was the stone which the town's name derived from—Cloch Shiurdain—the stone of Jordon, 'Cloch' being Gaelic for stone.

The town of Cloughjordon, County Tipperary, is an Irish town in the ancient province of Munster. It is on the county border of North Tipperary and County Offaly.

Jordon married Agnes Plantagenen and they had three sons and a daughter. Agnes was known to have had an affair with King John. Their daughter Elinor married Maurice Fitzmaurice, and it was while constructing their castle that Jordon was killed.

Jordon's eldest son, William de Marisco (born before 1213), is the first in the line described as of East Rasen in Lincolnshire. He first married Margery and they had two known sons,

William and John. He then married Matilda. Meanwhile, Lundy Island had been taken away from the de Mariscos but was gifted back to William in 1281. He survived to enjoy Lundy for fewer than three years. He had been predeceased by his son William.

His second son, John de Marisco, married Olive, daughter of Milo FitzDavid, the Baron of Iverk. They had two sons. The youngest, William, was summoned to King Edward I (reigned 1272–1307) at Berwick on Tweed, as a Lincolnshire Knight. Herbert de Marisco (de Mareys), the elder son, was a minor when Lundy Island was passed on to him by his father. In 1299 Herbert came of age and inherited back Lundy and the lands in Somerset, England, and their Irish lands.

The rebellion of 1321 resulted in the loss of Lundy Island to Hugh Dispenser. Herbert de Marisco again lodged a claim to Lundy and petitioned the King in 1322. He was summoned for Military Service in 1324. The day the order was made on Lundy Island, Herbert died, and his lands of which he was tenant in chief were again taken until his son and heir, Stephen, would prove his age, and make homage to the King. Herbert de Marisco (de Mareys) first married Sybilla, daughter and heiress of Walter de la Have, the Escheator of Ireland (manager of lands lapsed to the crown). They had three sons, Stephen, Walter and William. He next married Isobella, widow of Simon Roges and daughter of Sir John de Tracey of Woodcombe in Somerset, and they had a son, Nicholas.

In 1327 Stephen, the eldest son, made homage to King Edward and was given seisin of his father's lands. Three years later King Edward III took over the Government of the Kingdom. This was the end of the long hold of Lundy Island by the de Mariscos. William de Mareys, the younger son of Herbert, succeeded his elder brother Stephen de Marisco (de Mareys) and acquired his mother's Lincolnshire estate. He appears in Ireland in 1334–35. William married Mary, daughter of Raymond de Cantwell, and they had one known son, Thomas Mareys.

There is a change in the spelling of the de Marisco name with each new generation, and also a downturn in their wealth. Thomas Mareys is described only of Ingoldmells in Lincolnshire. The estates in Somerset, Ireland, and Lundy Island were lost from the de Marisco line. Their fortunes had dwindled, and this once-powerful family had moved from aristocracy to tenant farmer status.

The next generations resided in towns within Lincolnshire, Ingoldmells, Rothwell, Barrow-upon-Humber, Thornton Curtis, Goxhill, Kirmington and Aston Tirrold. The family name had gone from de Marisco to de Mareys, Mareys, and finally to Marris.

In the eleventh, twelfth, and thirteenth centuries, when there was much wealth in these families, they were very small. The next centuries saw larger families and a downturn in fortunes for most.

PART II

Modern Times: The Marris family

A window of time allows us to move on from the 1400s to the 1700s. This period brought about many changes. The name 'de Marisco' had gone through several changes and was now 'Marris'. Fortunes had disappeared and this once-powerful family had become of peasantry and yeomanry status. Geographically, their lives had taken them away from the south-west of England to Lincolnshire in the east. Many settled within a 12-mile radius of the Humber River and our next family lived at Barton-upon-Humber. This is their story.

6

Thomas Marris and the North Lincolnshire Bank

Thomas Marris Jnr, born in 1757, was the eleventh child of fifteen children. His father, also called Thomas Marris, and his wife Elizabeth Ostler, had built up a healthy fortune, owning farmland and buildings in Barton-upon-Humber. They bought a property in Priestgate in 1774, demolished it and built Cobb Hall (Figure 10) in its place. This building, along with many other properties, passed on to Thomas Jnr upon the death of his parents. This left him a very wealthy man. (Most of his siblings had died in infancy.)

Figure 10. Cobb Hall in Barton-upon-Humber, built by Thomas Marris

Thomas Marris Jnr was married twice, and had thirteen children. He first married Helen Grayburn. His second wife, Jane Hildyard whom he married in 1792, was a descendant of the Plantagenet roll of Royal Blood. Such was the scale of land owned by Thomas Marris, that at the enclosure of 1791–1793 he was awarded 162 acres, 3 rods and 12 perches, and was the eighth largest landowner in Barton at the time. He was recorded in a trade directory of 1791 as an attorney who often worked on cases of bankruptcy. In the trade directory of 1811 he was recorded as a Banker.

Thomas had become an extremely wealthy man, of high honour, and unimpeachable integrity. He was an attorney by profession and resided in Baysgath House. Along with a Mr Nicholson, also an attorney of great respectability, they formed the North Lincolnshire Bank at Barton-upon-

Humber. The bank was one of issue and deposit. They opened a branch of their bank in London, and Messrs Boldero, Lussington and Co were their agents. So great was the confidence in Marris and Nicholson, that their banknotes were preferred to the notes of every other local bank. Indeed, they were considered equal to gold, or Bank of England paper. Not only were their notes ranked high in public esteem (Figure 11), but the bank was used by local business, and for temporary purposes. There was scarcely a gentleman, a business man, or a large farmer in the town or district who didn't have an account with them. Trustees and executors lodged money in their hands. Almost every person in the neighbourhood who had managed to save a little money, through frugality, took it there for security.

Figure 11. Banknote issued by North Lincolnshire Bank

Thomas Marris owned the Market Lane Mill in 1810, which milled corn into flour. Later, it became a chalk (whiting) mill that converted many tons of stone into chalk.

The bank was well managed, extensively used, and flourished, and the proprietors held the social position of first class country gentlemen.

The bank had enjoyed prosperous times until 13 January 1812, when their London agents Bolero, Lushington & Co failed, leaving Marris and Nicholson indebted to them for 34,000 pounds (approx. $1,155,000 in today's value.)

The North Lincolnshire Bank, and Thomas Marris's bankruptcy in 1812, was one of the most disastrous financial events in the history of Barton and the surrounding areas. Claims of over 200,000 pounds were proved against the joint estate by 1000 individuals. The disaster didn't stop there, however, as many of the working men, local shops, and private individuals had many of the one pound notes issued by the bank, which had suddenly became worthless.

Thomas Marris was part of a group of wealthy farmers in 1810 who had commissioned a portrait which was aimed to promote those associated with the 'new agriculture' in Lincolnshire. Plans for a print of the painting were abandoned when Mr Marris's bank collapsed in 1812.

(At the George Inn in Barton upon Humber) 'The following estates, the property of Thomas Marris and Richard Nicholson, bankrupts, on days to be hereafter appointed, in the following lots: Lot 1 – An exceedingly good Mansion House in Barton, lately occupied by Mr Thomas Marris, with walled gardens, well stocked with fruit trees, a stove green house, a gardeners house, fish ponds well stocked with Carp, very good stables, beast houses, a barn, and every convenience necessary, with forty three acres of land adjourning, beautifully enclosed and ornamented with plantations. Lot 11 – A most excellent farm, called the Grange, containing 207 acres of land in a ring fence, with excellent buildings in the centre. Lot 111 – A whiting mill, with shades adjourning. Also some other houses and land to be divided onto lots, of which notice will be given, when the day of sale is appointed.

This was all reported in the *Hull Packet* on 25 February 1812.

The mansion house in question was Baysgath House which Thomas purchased in 1806. The farm called The Grange was situated between Horkstow and Saxby All Saints. The whiting mill was Kings Garth Mill in Barton Place Market, which he had built around 1810. Again, this was an indication of the size of Thomas Marris's wealth at the time. Some of the valuable livestock on his farm was sold by auction on 27 and 28 May 1812, again being reported in the *Hull Packet*. There were upwards of 130 valuable rams of different ages. There was an auction of valuable household furniture, thirty dozen bottles of excellent port, sherry and wines, quality china and bed linen, and a collection of valuable books.

The final dividend was reported in the *London Gazette* of 27 July 1858. In total, the creditors were paid 9s 1/4d in the pound, stretching over 46 years. Thomas Marris's estate paid his private creditors in full. He became a member of the Old Friends Society and never lost his personal and commercial integrity. After his bankruptcy, an old servant paid his monthly contributions for him, again showing that he was still held in high esteem.

In 1856, a historian of the time, J Ball Esq, (*Ball's Social History and Antiquities of Barton*) wrote of Mr Marris, "A wealthy man of high honour, unimpeachable integrity and universally esteemed".

Thomas Walkden, in 1812, supported his friend through a business incident that was described as, "the most disastrous event in the annals of Barton." Because their London agents, Boldero, Lushington & Co. had failed, leaving Marris and Nicholson indebted to them, causing loss and ruin staring the bulk of the inhabitants sternly in the face, Thomas Marris was found dead whilst living in an outhouse at his son Robert's home in Leicester in 1848.

This disaster shook the public faith in the banking system in the local area, and lead to local people hoarding their savings in their own keeping—in houses in tins, under beds, and one former depositor kept his in a glass rolling pin, but some unscrupulous person unfortunately stole the money. There were many business people in Barton and the surrounding areas, between 1812 and 1858, who went bankrupt. Thus there was another era of wealth gained and lost.

7

Reverend George Marris: The English connection

Another branch of the Marris family came from Thornton Curtis. This is a family that spans the globe. Some members stayed in the Mother Country but others sailed across the seas to seek their fortunes in Australia and New Zealand.

George Marris (b 1780–81) was ordained into the Ministry in the connection of the Countess of Huntington in 1816. He became the first minister in a new Chapel in Congleton, the Zion Chapel, where he remained until 1825. George then became minister at Aston Tirrold for the next seventeen years.

George married Sarah Murrell. Sarah was the daughter of George Alexander Murrell but was adopted by her Aunt dowager, Viscountess Barrington. They had seven children.

George and Sarah's three sons were a new generation whose diversified lives led them to separate parts of the world and, in some cases, into businesses that led to boom and bust.

George Marris, the youngest son of the above, was born in 1829 and as a young man moved to Birmingham, which was where he was to make his fortune. Birmingham by the mid eighteenth century was the fastest growing industrial town in the land, and became the 'city of a thousand trades'. The brass industry was the most important of all the many trades.

Two years after moving there, he started trading on his own account as a bedstead manufacturer and retailer at 29 Bull Street. Further down Bull Street, another young man, John Cadbury, also had a new business, Cadburys (Cadburys chocolate), a high-end business for the wealthy.

George met and married Miss Sarah Swindell Suffield. Her father John Suffield had an important retail and wholesale haberdashery business, also in Bull Street. Sarah's sister, Mabel Suffield, married Arthur Tolkien, a music and piano teacher who had moved from London to Birmingham. They emigrated to South Africa where their son, John Ronald Reuel Tolkien, was born in Bloemfontain. When John was three years old, his mother brought him and his younger brother back to Birmingham to visit their grandparents. That was the last time he saw his father who died. They stayed on in England. JRR Tolkien wrote *The Hobbit* and *Lord of the Rings*.

George's business prospered and became known as Marris Emporium. He stole the top furniture designer, Mr Norton, from Chamberlain, King & Jones, and they expanded their business and moved to Corporation Street.

A heading in a local paper at the time read:

Sotheby's sale of the contents of Benacre Hall achieves record 8.3 million pounds, the highest total ever for a country house content sale in the United Kingdom—the highest price paid today, was for a fine 19th century satin sycamore and marquetry cylinder bureau, by Messrs Marris & Norton of Corporation Street, Birmingham. The piece, decorated throughout with neo-classical motifs, sold for 32,700 pounds, over four times its pre-sale low estimate of 8,000 pounds.

Unlucky for himself, Norton at length bought Mr Marris out of business, and Mr Marris retired on a very considerable competence. Norton then floated a big company and took in shareholders. Disaster struck when the business burnt down and all the shareholders lost their invested money. Hence, the company dropped into obliviation.

In the meantime, George started up a new company. George and Sarah had twelve children. By now he was a very wealthy man and educated his children well, sending them abroad to further their education. This is where he invested his money, in a good education for his children.

George Jnr (born 1857), his eldest son, worked with his father in the new firm making brass founders, stampers and pierces. When George Snr died, a loan against the family home, used for his business, was recalled, which put George Jnr into liquidation. George Snr had put another son into business, but it too had failed, so a lot of the family money was gone.

Later, the business reformed as Marris Limited and gradually picked up. In the 1920s his youngest son Richard joined him. They began diversifying from beds and fern pot bases, and designed their own brand name, 'Sirram', which is Marris spelt backwards. This appeared on their picnic sets. The first Sirram Volcano Kettle appeared in the late 1920s. Later the Marris's switched from the copper and brass kettles to spun aluminium. (Figure 12)

Figure 12. Sirram kettle

There is a record that there was a meeting between one

of the Marris family members in Birmingham and a New Zealander, almost certainly John Ashley Hart, who started the Thermette Company in New Zealand.

This report, in an English *Autocar* magazine of 1970 stated: "Desmo Ltd have purchased the Sirram picnic division of Hawker & Marris Sales Ltd. Brexton Ltd, a division of Desmo, will now market all Sirram products, which will continue as a separate range." It appears that the company of Hawker & Marris closed down in 1970. Since then, many companies around the world have brought out a modern version of the Sirram Kettle.

Ada Marris (b 1856), George Snr's eldest daughter, was educated in Germany and taught at girls' schools in Edgbaston and Hastings. She joined the London Missionary Society and sailed for Benares, India, in 1882, where she worked for the next thirty-five years. Ada returned to England and helped in the training of would-be missionaries, before settling into writing. She wrote *Through Eastern Windows: Life stories of an Eastern City* published in 1919. Her second book *Woman's Needs in India: A Litany of Help* was published in 1920. Ada remained a spinster and was troubled with severe arthritis. She died aged 88 years.

Another of George Snr's sons, Walter, was educated at Amersham, then went to a firm of accountants in Birmingham. His father bought him a partnership in a London printing firm, but this was not successful. When Walter's wife died and left him with a young daughter, he left her in the care of her grandparents and emigrated to Perth in Australia. He joined Swan Brewery Company and became a senior representative. He later married and had three sons. Thus a branch of the Marris family was now established in Australia.

Nora Murrell Marris (b 1861) was George Snr's fourth child. She was handicapped by partial deafness from early childhood. Nora became friends with Beatrice Chamberlain, daughter of Joseph Chamberlain. She wrote his first biography, *The Right Honourable Joseph Chamberlain: The Man and The Statesman* which was published in 1890. Joseph Chamberlain, the son of a shopkeeper, was a British politician and statesman who made his career in Birmingham, first as a manufacturer of screws, then as a notable Mayor of that city. This was where the two families' lives connected. Nora died tragically, while driving home during a wartime blackout.

The youngest son, William Marris, was educated at King Edward VI Grammar and the Medical School in Birmingham. He obtained a London MD, then became a ship's doctor for a merchant shipping line and was a civil surgeon in the Boer War in 1899. He then settled into a general practice at Kings Heath, Birmingham.

All George Snr's children were highly educated and intelligent. The other girls were involved in teaching and nursing. The youngest daughter, Isobel, was secretary of the Woman's Suffrage Association from 1900 and in 1907 became a secretary in the Duty and Discipline Movement, visiting South Africa. In her later years she became involved with the Film & Entertainment Censorship.

Further down through George and Sarah's generations came academics, writers, professors and economists.

Robin Marris (b 1924) was an RAF pilot in the last years of the Second World War. He spent two years in the English Treasury and two years with the United Nations in Geneva. He returned to Cambridge University in 1951 as a lecturer (later as a reader) in the economics faculty, posts he held for 25 years. In 1976 he moved to a chair at the University of Maryland in the United States, and in 1981 he returned to Birkbeck College, University of London. Robin had a lively mind and warm personality. He wore Carnaby suits and was a witty, charming and generous person. Although he was very clever academically, his social life was in tatters. Attracted to, and attracted by women, he broke up with three wives in succession. He had three children before he met and married his third wife, Anne Fairclough Mansfield. Anne was also an academic and the only child of Michael Mansfield, a United States Senator from 1961–1977, who was the longest-serving Senate Majority Leader. Robin and Anne had a daughter and this marriage ended.

Robin Marris wrote many books, among them were: *Ending Poverty* published in 1999, *How to Save the Underclass* published in 1997, and *Managerial Capitalism in Retrospect* in 1998. He was an influential economist and academic, noted for his work on outstanding corporations. Robin Lapthorn Marris died in 2012.

Robin's only son, Toby Marris (b 1965), was the skipper of the sailing schooner the Jolie Brise. He teaches students from the Dauntsey's School in Wiltshire to sail offshore and races in the Fastnet Race, one of the biggest challenges in English yachting.

Peter Marris, born 1928 in London, was a cousin of Robin Marris. He served in the military as a British Colonial Officer in Africa then returned to England to study sociology at Cambridge University. In 1955 he joined the Institute of Community Studies in London. In his earlier years as a scholar, he published studies on widowhood in London, slum clearance in Nigeria, the lives of African businessmen in Kenya, and poverty programs in the United States.

Peter Marris married Delores Hayden, a Yale Professor, and they had a daughter, Laura. He was a professor of urban planning at UCLA in America from 1976–1991, and also a lecturer in City and Regional Planning at UC Berkeley and at the Massachusetts Institute of Technology. In all, Peter wrote fourteen books: *African City Life* published in 1961, *Widows and their Families* published in 1958, and *The Politics of Uncertainty* in 1996 to name a few. Peter died in 2007. He was the brother of Tyrrell Marris, one of the Marris family members who kept the 'Marris Journal' updated.

8

Charles Marris:
The New Zealand connection

Charles Marris (b 1832) was the Reverend George Marris's youngest son. He practised as an accountant in Birmingham. He first married Rebecca Knowles and they lived at Dudley Road, Wolverhampton. In 1858, Rebecca was dying of uterine cancer and was very sick. In October of that year, Elizabeth Fearcombe—who had returned from India—also lived on Dudley Road with her Uncle Henry Fearcombe and gave birth to a son out of wedlock. The father was not listed on the birth certificate but four years later, in 1862, Charles and Elizabeth married. (Had a little scandal appeared?)

There was no record of what happened to Elizabeth, but in 1872 Charles Marris married Jessie Sophia Sinclair and they had eleven children. Charles was a well-known accountant in Birmingham but suffered from poor health. So the family left the mother country and arrived in New Zealand in 1884, settling in Wanganui (Figure 13). An advertisement in a Wellington newspaper of the time shows Charles advertising as an accountant, so it is not known if he practised there or in Wanganui. However, given that their next child was born in Birmingham, England in 1887, their stay in the colony was short-lived.

His eldest son, William, stayed on in New Zealand to finish his education, going to Canterbury College in Christchurch (which was later to become Canterbury University). William was a contemporary of Ernest Rutherford, the mathematical physicist. Rutherford received the undergraduate maths prize each year from 1890–92. However, records show that in the first year, he shared it with William Marris, a classicist, and in the second and third years, he was beaten by, then equal with, Marris. The prize was awarded to Rutherford, however, because a student could only hold one scholarship and William had also won the classics scholarship, so he took that. And so began a distinguished career.

In 1905 William married Eleanor Ferguson but she died the following year in India after giving birth to their son, Adam. William Marris became Civil Service Commissioner of the Transvaal and deputy chairman of the Committee on the Central South African Railways. He did not return to India for several years and instead went on a world tour through Canada, Australia and New Zealand, organising the Round Table Groups with a man named Curtis. The Round

Table, founded in 1909, was an association of organisations promoting closer union between Britain and its self-governing colonies.

Figure 13. Jessie Marris and family

Back in India in 1912, William became a member of the

Dunbar Executive Committee and, later, secretary to the Home Department of the Government of India. In 1916, he became Inspector General of the Police, and the following year, joint secretary to the Governor of India. In 1921 he was knighted, and became Sir William Marris (Figure 14). He was Governor of Assam 1921–22, then Governor of the United Province. Among other honours, he was given the KCSI (Knights Commander of the Order of the Star of India). Later, Sir William returned to England.

After his retirement from active administration, which brought him additional honours, he became Principal of Armstrong College in Newcastle upon Tyne from 1925–1937, Vice Chancellor of Durham University, and a Governor of the Royal Agricultural College in Cirencester to 1945.

Sir William was involved with an organisation called the Milner Group. He brought into the Group, from the Indian Civil Service, Malcolm Hailey (since 1936, Lord Hailey). The Milner Group controlled the Rhodes fortune after Cecil Rhodes' death in 1902. Cecil Rhodes acquired the major gold and diamond mines of Southern Africa and used his wealth to pursue his dreams. In 1891 he established a secret society, and when he realised that he would not live to see his vision fulfilled, he left his vast fortune to the Rhodes Trust. This was to fund his secret society and the Rhodes Scholarship Fund.

William Marris authored and translated several publications including *The Odes of Horace* by Horace, translated in 1912 by William Marris; *The Iliad of Homer* by Homer, translated by William Marris; and several other works. These were published in London and New York. Sir William Marris died in Gloucestershire on 12 December 1945.

Figure 14. Sir William Marris

Adam Denzil Marris, William's only child, was born in India in 1906 and educated in England. After graduating from Winchester School and Trinity College in Oxford, he went to work with Lazard Brothers Banking. There was no doubt that this position was obtained through his father's association with Mr Brand who at the time was manager of Lazard Banking. Adam remained with the banking firm for ten years, but at the outbreak of war he joined the Ministry of Economics & Warfare for a year. He then joined the All Souls Foreign Affairs Group, an unofficial discussion group which was monopolizing the British Embassy in Washington. He joined the Embassy as First Secretary, and later as Counsellor to the Embassy from 1940–1945.

After the war, he was British Foreign Office representative on the Economic Committee for Europe, as Secretary General. In 1946, he returned to Lazard Brothers to become managing director of Lazard Frères Bank. Adam married Miss Barbara Waterfield and they had two daughters and a son, David.

David Marris (b 1942) was a former Army Officer, who went on to become an executive in an international bank. He met his future wife, Claire, while holidaying in Nairobi. Some of the scenes from the movie *Out of Africa*, with Meryl Streep and Robert Redford, were shot on a ranch in the Rift Valley where Claire's family had lived for generations. After spells around the world with his job, including Barbados, Adam and Claire settled in Norfolk in the UK. They bought a splendid Georgian home called 'Tunstead' where they retired. They had two daughters.

Charles Marris's second son, Carl Murrell Marris, was born in England in 1875. As boy, he was put to work in the Midland Bank but he hated it and ended up running away to sea. Having been at sea from the ages of fourteen to twenty-three, his sailings were well-documented on his application for his second mates' examination which he took in Liverpool in 1898. He listed service in no fewer than fifteen ships.

Carl clearly had ambitions to improve his fortunes and decided for his own betterment to study at the Gifford's Navigation School in Grey Street, Wellington, New Zealand. He sat and passed his examination for first mate in the spring of 1900 (recorded in the New Zealand *Evening Post*) and on 7 June 1901, little more than a year later, he received his Master's Certificate from the New Zealand Government. Carl was next cited in April 1903 when outbound from Wellington as second officer of the *Janet Nicholl*, a ship with mostly Malay crew. At that time, Carl Marris was definitely settled in Malaya and in family history records there is mention in 1909 of a daughter by Carl and Wan Zaharah, a Princess of Pattani. Carl had taken the Muslim faith of his wife. He also mentioned her in a letter to writer Joseph Conrad. "I have to leave England, and get home to my Princess wife and daughter, for they want me to return."

Carl was the owner of the Archipelago trader, the *Araby*

Maid, and he traded around the Malaysian waters as well as gun-running to the Achinese. He had sailed with Joshua Lingard on the *Rajah Laut*.

Following Carl's own statement in his first letter to Joseph Conrad at the beginning of July 1909, both *A Portrait in Letters: Correspondence to and About Conrad* and the Cambridge Edition's introduction to Conrad's *Twixt Land & Sea* account for him as a New Zealander. Carl's words were, "My parents returned from New Zealand, of which colony I am a native."

This claim is incorrect as he was born in Aston, a ward of Birmingham, England, on 25 January 1875. He did, however, reside briefly in New Zealand with his parents as a youngster, aged about eight. He is referred to in this extract.

When Carl met Joseph Conrad in 1909, the soft eyed, black-bearded man with a dark complexion, brown eyes and tattoos on his arms, was in ill health. His sojourn in England having been an attempt to find better care, than that available in Penang. They discussed times at sea, and the adventures that had accompanied their separate lives.

(Source: *Conrad and Captain Marris: a biographical note*. Stape, J. H. & Niland, R. 1 Nov 2014 in : *The Conradian : The Journal of the Joseph Conrad Society* (UK). 39, 2, 21 p.)

Joseph Conrad (1857–1924) was a Polish author who wrote in English after settling in England. He was regarded as one of the greatest novelists in English, often writing stories and novels of a nautical nature. He dedicated his book *Twixt Land and Sea* to, "Captain CM Marris, Late Master and Owner of the Araby Maid, Archipelago Trader. In Memory of those old days of Adventure."

After this, he returned home to Pulo Tikus and told Conrad that he had seen some improvement in his health, but this was short-lived. Sometime after this, he again set out for England, only making it to Colombo, where he died on 15 May 1910. As witness, there is a memorial in the churchyard of St Peters at Cookley, Worcestershire.

Charles Marris's other children ventured afar. Roy Markham Marris (b 1880 in England) came to New Zealand aged four with his parents, then returned to England. He was an engraver by trade. At eighteen, he fought for England at the Boer War, then remained in South Africa with the Mounted Police for another three years. After travelling around the world, he settled in Invercargill, New Zealand, where he met and married Christian Watson. As it was the depression years, jobs were hard to get, so he went flax cutting. He would cycle to work on a Sunday night and cycle home again on a Saturday morning to spend the little spare time he had with his family. He had two sons, Alan and Dick, and three daughters, Vivienne, Hope and Joyce.

Alan Marris, the eldest of Roy's children, became a farmer and at different times owned several farms in Southland. He remained a bachelor and delved into buying and selling. The auctioneers welcomed him at the auctions as he seemed to buy all the junk that no-one wanted. At times his farm looked like a bombsite, but this didn't stop his bank account from growing. He had a kind heart and when tragedy struck his brother's family, he bought the family a home for the children and made sure they had money.

His brother, Dick, died in his early fifties, leaving behind a wife and eight children. Then one year later, two of the older boys drowned in Bluff harbour and this broke their mother's heart. When she passed away, she left behind six younger children. They were a poor family, so having the comfort of a mortgage-free home and money invested meant the remaining children could stay together as a family. This branch of the Marris family settled in Southland, and later branched into Otago.

Claude Thorneycroft Marris (b 1879 in Birmingham), emigrated to South Africa and made his money in the diamond fields. Eventually he was the equivalent of an Estates Bursar to Cape Town University.

The youngest son of Charles Marris, Alan Barrington Marris (b 1890), was killed in England in the First World War.

9

Henry M Marris:
The Australian connection

Henry Markham Marris, born in England in 1826, was the eldest son of the Reverend George Marris. He was a civil engineer by trade. Henry, with his wife Mary and their three sons, Charles, Henry and George, sailed from Liverpool in October 1862 on the ship Blue Jacket and arrived in Australia in January 1863.

Their eldest son, Charles Augustus Marris, born in Lincolnshire, married Agnes Reid Allan in Australia. Agnes was a lass from Glasgow. Charles was a law clerk and later became a school teacher in Australia. They had twelve children.

Charles' and Agnes's second eldest son, Charles Allan Marris, born in Melbourne in 1876, became a schoolteacher at

Ballarat and Ipswich. He was reputed to have represented Queensland at cricket, played tennis, and had an encyclopaedic knowledge of sports. Charles married Ethel Anderson Rivitt in Melbourne in 1900 and, in about 1904, they moved with the first of their children to Wellington, New Zealand, where Charles was a relieving teacher at Newtown School, and then Fernridge in Wairarapa.

Charles left teaching and became a journalist with the *Evening Post*, and in 1913 was appointed the *Post's* representative in the Parliamentary Press Gallery. The following year, Charles left Wellington to become associate editor on the *Christchurch Sun*. He was published regularly by the *Christchurch Press* under the pen name Percy Flage. After a decade in Christchurch, the family returned to Wellington where Charles became managing editor of the *New Zealand Times*. In 1928, Charles began his long association with the printer and publisher, Harry H Tombs, when he became literary editor of the prestigious quarterly journal, *Art in New Zealand*. He developed his own aspirations as a poet and short story writer. A poem by Charles signed 'Prestor John' was published in the *Canterbury University College Review* in 1931, alongside work by Denis Glover. He worked alongside, and helped, poets and writers like Robin Hyde and Dora Hagemeyer. Charles died in June 1947, survived by his wife, four sons and a daughter.

Three of Charles sons were involved in writing and

publishing books. This has been a prominent gene, passed down through the Marris lineage.

Charles' second son, Eric Charles Marris, and his wife bought a rundown magazine called the *New Zealand Financial Times* and turned it into a success. Eric wrote *NZ Investment Guide*, a complete handbook for investors, and a hardcover in 1959 of *NZ Financial Times*. Eric received an OBE and was a director of New Zealand Forest Products Ltd and chairman of Clyde Engineering.

Eric's son, Michael Eric Marris (b 1945) lives in Auckland and is a psychologist who has written several books including *Teenagers: A Parent's Guide for the 90s* (1996). (Figure 15)

In 2010, there was a rare book auctioned by Bethune's at Webb's Rare Book sale, called *Pixie Pranks*. This rare children's book had a reserve of $50.00 and sold above the reserve. The author of this book was Bruce Marris, a son of Charles Marris. Not only did he write this book, but also did the humorous illustrations, showing a group of mischievous pixies getting up to all sorts of tricks at a fair.

Guy Digby Marris, Charles' oldest son (b 1906) researched the history of the *Bounty* mutineers. In 1936 he wrote extended papers on this and they are mounted inside the back cover of *The Court Martial of the Bounty Mutineers*. This is about fact versus fiction, the story of Bligh and Christian regarding Pitcairn Island.

Figure 15. Michael Marris

Guy's son, Guy Junior (b 1962), has spent much of his adult life outside of New Zealand, travelling in remote areas and later working in the nature conservation and sustainable development field. He began his working life in the 1980s, surveying the biodiversity of New Zealand's state forests, followed by several years as an officer with the New Zealand Wildlife Service working on endangered species recovery programs. A love of photography then led him to work for the TVNZ Natural History Unit in Dunedin as a cameraman-director for documentaries and children's wildlife programmes. Following a deep desire to assist in conservation efforts in the developing tropical world, he joined the New Zealand Volunteer Service Abroad program in 1997 as a technical advisor to a World Bank protected area management project in Laos.

Figure 16. Guy Marris

Since that time Guy, has remained working overseas in nature conservation and sustainable development projects, focusing on protected areas in South East Asia, and in eastern and western Africa. His last appointment was in Sierra Leone managing a forest conservation and climate change mitigation project for the RSPB of the UK. He was published in 2008 as a co-author of *A Responsible Tourism Guide to Cambodia, Laos and Vietnam*. (Figure 16)

Another son of Guy Marris Snr is John Marris whom I will come back to later, as his story is a fitting end to the history of the de Marisco descendants.

10

Lincolnshire Marris branch: West Coast settlers

This branch of the Marris family lived in Kirton-in-Lindsey and was of yeoman stock. They had suffered hardship during the depressed British economy of 1830s and early 1840s. This is their story.

In England, by the middle of the nineteenth century, the fortunes of the Marris family and its offshoots were moving into new ventures, away from the humdrum of the joinery trade, and the simple respectability it provided. Some were on their way to becoming prosperous business owners, while other members of the family were going to experience hard times.

Some of the menfolk died young, leaving widows with children. Other families lost both parents and, for some, life was going to be nothing other than a struggle. Ann, the widow of Brady Marris, is listed as a pauper in the 1851 English census. Maria and John Barnaby Marris, the children of William and Rebecca, had lost both of their parents very young and, as orphans, had had to be put into the workhouse at Goole where both were described as paupers. Maria survived the gruelling workhouse and by 1859 was back in Kirton-in-Lindsey where she had an illegitimate child. But this child, whom she called Rebecca after her mother, only lived for seventeen days. She went on to marry but had no more children. John also survived the rigours of the Goole workhouse and by 1867 had emigrated to Victoria, Australia.

While the British branch of the family was undergoing its trials and tribulations, the more enterprising members of the family had emigrated to the Australian Colonies. The mass exodus from England and Ireland to the 'New World' was in full swing and it was this exciting 'happening' that the Marris family wanted to be part of.

John Barnaby Marris (born 1804 at Kirton-in-Lindsey) became a joiner in his teenage years. At the age of 21, he met Susanna Langdon Preston. The couple married in 1825. It is thought in some quarters that Susanna was a member of the aristocracy and was in fact Lady Susanna Langton Preston of Preston Hall. This story claims that John Marris was then a stable hand at Preston Hall, but that his attention strayed from the horses in his care to the beautiful daughter of the house. We're not sure whether it's true or not!

John and Susanna however did have a big family, following the traditions of the nineteenth century. They had six children born in England whom they brought out to Port Phillip, Melbourne, Australia. They came over from England on the ship *John Bull* in late 1839 and had a further two children in Australia.

John's brother Thomas Marris emigrated with his wife to Melbourne in about 1850 on the ship the *Medway*. In his early years in Melbourne, Thomas moved up in the world from a humble tailor to a prosperous self-employed hotelkeeper, operating the aptly-named Lincoln Inn at 29 Queensberry Street, North Melbourne. This hotel still operates from this site and has been updated several times. It was thought it was named by Thomas after his home county of Lincolnshire in England. Thomas built a considerable fortune in this business and owned a number of properties. Thomas died in 1865 at Footscray, Melbourne, in some sort of accident. His wife Harriet operated the hotel for some years before their son John took over.

In the 1850s, Victoria was a booming, bustling colony. It continued to boom despite losing more than a third of its population to the goldfields of Ballarat and Bendigo. Victoria thrived as its hinterland produced fine merino wool which was exported back to the mother country. The streets of Ballarat may have been thought to be paved with gold, but the vast majority of those who chased it found only disappointment, gaining at best enough money to survive.

By the early 1860s, however, enough was enough, for the Australian colonies had outlived their usefulness. A number of members of the Marris family had shown enterprise in travelling across the world from the mother country. Now, with the next generation, there were pastures greener to seek.

It was time to move on, and the fledging colony of New Zealand beckoned. Gold was being discovered in Central Otago. Now Dunedin had become a prosperous centre. Once in Dunedin, the Marris brothers settled down and were joined a short while later by William's wife, who had stayed on in Australia. William remained in Dunedin from 1865–1882 and became a property owner, his property being on High Street.

John Marris Jnr moved on to Southland to manage a timber mill at Makarewa. However, the lure of gold beckoned, so the Marris brothers decided to follow the gold, first to Central Otago and Hokitika, then in 1868 to Charleston on the West Coast of New Zealand. They came to the realisation that the biggest fortunes on the goldfields tended to be made not by the miners, but by those trades that supplied them. It was in Charleston that the Marris brothers found their niche.

Their first major business venture was the purchase of the Nile Stream Sawmill Company. The new company became known as W & J Marris Ltd. The greatest asset of the mill was the timber. But the sawmill was not the only business interest of the Marris brothers. William in particular seemed to have an eye for business and a great vision. In 1868 he established the Nile Cement, Gold and Water Company. Regardless of whether this company ever produced any gold, water or cement, it served as a vehicle for William to raise capital for other businesses. Almost all of these companies disappeared as quickly as they appeared and William's company seems to have been no exception.

The timber market was booming, but tragedy was to strike on a personal front during the Charleston years. William's wife, Lauretta, died in 1872, aged 39, and was buried in the then Charleston cemetery. Not for long though, as the vicious seas began to eat away at the land, and Lauretta's body, along with many others, had to be exhumed and reburied in the new Nile Hill cemetery.

While death is part of the natural life cycle, so is birth, and while William's family was ending, his brother John's was beginning. John married Amelia Lehane, an Irish woman who had come from Bantry in Ireland. They had five children.

By 1873 the Charleston years were coming to an end. John and his family moved to Westport and not long after that, William also moved there and the timber empire of the brothers expanded. By this time the Marris brothers were regarded as businessmen rather than sawmillers.

A window of time allows us to move on to the next generation. In 1907, there were in fact twenty-three sawmills operating in Buller. S & J Marris were operating at

Mokihinui, about 27 miles north of Westport. They held cutting rights over 400 acres of crown and private land. Most of their output was Rimu. The company held a further lease over 200 acres of crown land one and a half miles from the railway in Mokihinui.

Most of the timber was processed into sleepers and transported to all parts of the country for the rapidly expanding rail network, or used in bridge construction. Coal was rapidly becoming Buller's major industry. The mill did not just turn out bulk timber, but produced flooring, match lining, architraves, mouldings and skirtings. The future of the sawmilling industry looked assured, but for one cloud on the horizon. This was the continued high importation of Oregon timber from overseas. It was claimed that if the Government did not clamp down on these huge imports, sawmillers would eventually go to the wall. Some sawmillers in Buller, it was claimed, were running at a loss, only to be kept alive by their banks.

The Marris operations were to continue for more than another twenty years. It was nature, in the form of the 1929 Murchison Earthquake, which effectively ended the operation.

While the Marris family sawmill may have been struggling in the 1920s, it may literally have had a fortune in its possession just waiting to be picked up. It could have made the family rich beyond their wildest dreams—but nobody knew about it.

Just what was this potential wealth? It was not timber or coal, but 'moissanite'.

Moissanite is a rare mineral which is a combination of silica and carbon, closely related to diamonds. Although not quite as valuable, it is used in imitation diamond rings with its estimated value about two thirds of that of a diamond. Scientists have attempted for many years to discover how moissanite forms. It was thought some came from meteorites which smashed into the earth's surface, and some were thought to be formed deep underground. However, these views were proved dramatically wrong when the largest block of this mineral ever found was discovered in Buller, in the firebox of the wood-fired boiler at the Marris sawmill.

After the mill was closed down in the late 1920s, it gently rotted away during the next decade. With the threat of war in 1939 there was talk about reopening the mill and the plant was cleaned up. It was during this process that what looked like a large glass slipper was discovered which had fallen off an even larger mass that was stuck to the back of the boilers. Syd Marris kept the mineral slipper as a curiosity with no idea of its value. After his death it apparently passed on to another family.

Later, when a piece was analysed at Auckland University and was revealed to be moissanite, there was a flurry of interest to find the remainder of it, and the boiler it had come from. But it had long disappeared, covered by undergrowth. The specimen itself was about seventeen centimetres long and about seven centimetres wide, and was a beautiful blue colour. It is believed that the timber used for firing the old boiler was Kahikatea and Rimu slabs from logs which may have been dragged overland where the silicon-rich soil had become embedded in the timber. No trace has ever been found of the original large mass of moissanite.

In the 1920s Syd Marris had got to know Francis Carter, the boss of the then Carter Company, through business and Lodge contacts. He somehow convinced Carter of the new phenomenon—not timber, but coal, the famous 'Black Diamonds' used to fire trains, ships and factories around the world. A company was formed with several shareholders. The venture went ahead but it soon became clear that there would be little or no return and they narrowly escaped bankruptcy when the coal enterprise collapsed.

However, Marris and Carter set up Granite Creek Sawmilling Company and after the coal collapse, this company expanded into cutting timber around Karamea. Syd was a hard taskmaster on his employees, but he managed the sawmill efficiently and economically. After Syd's death in 1936 the company began to struggle. Carter came down several times to close the mill, but didn't have the heart to put the men off. The mill wound up in 1971, just short of 50 years in operation.

A family landmark, in the form of a significant landform, is Marris Peak. At 4365 feet above sea level, it is a prominent feature in the mountains between the north branch of the

Mokihinui River and Little Wanganui. This is a fitting tribute to the Marris family, who helped shaped the history of the wild West Coast of New Zealand.

Only a few Marris families remain on the West Coast since much of the industry has disappeared. This has been brought about by political correctness, and probably the recent tragedies in the coal mining sector have added to these woes. Timber milling and mining are sadly a bygone era. These industries were the West Coast's bread and butter.

The West Coast Marris's have now gone full circle as some have gone to work in Australia where once a new life beckoned their ancestors. Others have moved on to greener pastures, away from the Coast.

John Marris, a descendant of the West Coast Marris family, has been the curator of Lincoln University's Entomology Research Collection for more than twenty years. John's research focus is on insect taxonomy—describing and naming new species, primarily beetles. His work has taken him to some unusual destinations in search of rare and unusual insects. This includes spending a month on the remote, sub-Antarctic Antipodes Islands, several trips to the Chatham Islands, and most recently to the mountain tops of the Southern Alps.

John has several insect species names in his honour, so the Marris name will live on in the world of entomology at least. A word from John: "I like to think that I, and the

Marris name, have gained a level of immortality from these species names, even if in the rather obscure world of insect taxonomy." This beetle, 'Syrphetodes marrisi' (Figure 17), is a new species from Kahurangi National Park and not too far removed from the West Coast Marris haunts.

Figure 17. 'Syrphetodes marrisi', a new species of beetle from Kahurangi National Park. *Photographed by John Marris*

11

Lincolnshire Marris branch: Nelson settlers

Sometimes family tragedies were a factor behind families leaving England. We will now follow the life of William Marris whose wife left him for another, leaving William with a young daughter, Emma. He hired a governess to be Emma's charge and they travelled to Nelson, New Zealand.

William Marris was born in 1825 in Lincolnshire. He left England with his new wife Betsy Utting, who was said to be little Emma's governess. In 1863 William, Betsy and Emma arrived in Nelson on the ship *Electra*. After arriving in New Zealand they had two children John (b 1864) and Frances (b 1866).

William bought a store in Waimea Road and had owned it for just a little over three years when he died in 1869. Betsy struggled to run the shop after William's death, as the bank wanted to foreclose, but she persuaded them to let her trade and she did so successfully. In November 1871 Betsy married a William Walker, a widower, and they had four children. In 1879 William Walker died and Betsy continued to run the shop until her son John was old enough to help her.

John Marris went into the building trade and, at 20 years old, worked for Fleming & Sons who were cabinet makers and undertakers. When John was 30 he married Emily Black and in 1917 he was elected to the Nelson City Council. He also built the little Anglican Church in 1889.

Several generations later, John Stone Marris (b 1923), who fought in the Second World War, earned the citation Distinguished Flying Cross. He completed many missions against such targets as Munich, Politz and Nuremburg. John was a farmer in the Nelson region.

John Marris also had the writing gene. He wrote *Tommy the Maori and Teapot*, which outlines events leading to the attack by Te Puoho on the Ngaitara Pa of Waimea. He also wrote a book called *Marris of Nelson and Lincolnshire, 1762–2003*.

12

Pioneering Marlborough winemaking family: John and Brent Marris

John Marris (1940–2014) and his son Brent (b 1962) are one of the pioneer winemaking families of world renown in the Marlborough region.

John is the son of Guy Marris, mentioned earlier in this book. John began his working life as a shepherd at the Picton freezing works, then became a stock agent. He brokered the land sales that became the Marlborough vineyard of pioneer wine company, Montana Wines. "I sold them nine farms in ten days, and virtually overnight Montana doubled the land values in the province, from $250 to $500 an acre," said John Marris who was a Pyne, Gould, Guinness land agent.

John Marris then began to establish the vineyard for Montana

Wines in Marlborough. He became one of Marlborough's first contract grape growers before developing one of the largest apple orchards and pack houses in the region.

In 1983 Brent gained a winemaking and viticultural degree, Bachelor of Applied Science in Oenology, from Adelaide's Roseworthy Agricultural College, South Australia. This made him Marlborough's first born and raised winemaker.

In 1998 John partnered with son Brent and his wine brand, Wither Hills. They jointly converted the apple pack house into the winery that it is today. John ran the vineyards and Brent focussed on winemaking and wine sales. They sold Wither Hills winery in 2002, but Brent remained managing director and chief winemaker for a further four years. (Figure 18)

Figure 18. Wither Hills Winery, Marlborough, New Zealand

John had a superb vision and a clear eye to the future potential of the Marlborough region. He developed residential and commercial property, including the Westwood retail development in Springlands. He also founded a truck diagnostics technology company, run by his two sons in New Zealand and the United States.

Brent's next step was founding Marisco Vineyards in 2003, with his wife Rosemary. The initial 650-acre vineyard is situated in the Waihopai Valley on the banks of the Waihopai River. Flowing over three distinct, ancient riverbed terraces, the fruit variation and complexity this site offers is something winemakers only dream about. (Figure 19)

Figure 19. Marisco Vineyards, Marlborough, New Zealand

Marisco Vineyards has developed into another internationally-successful wine company. With 600 acres of vines planted, and a 'new generation' winery built on site, the company is producing hundreds of thousands of cases of wine a year with half being sold into the UK market. (Figure 20)

Figure 20. Inside the Marisco winery. *Photographed by Christopher D. Thompson*

Brands include The Ned named after the tallest peak in the Wither Hills, an iconic symbol of Marlborough. In 2012, in the UK, The Ned Sauvignon Blanc won the Decanter World Wine Awards international trophy for the World's Best Sauvignon Blanc. The Ned has won in excess of 100 gold medals and trophies since its inception in 2006.

When Brent discovered his intriguing family lineage, the ancestral link to Lundy Island and the scandalous ancestors, he sent his creative director, Chris Thompson, to the island of Lundy. Chris was helicoptered out to Lundy, some ten minutes' flight from Bideford in Devon. He spent five days wandering the island, photographing its many moods, flora and fauna. His evenings were spent in the island's pub, the Marisco Tavern (Figure 21), poring over all the books and articles in the tavern's library, seeking out the history and stories that later became the foundation for the wine brand, The Kings Series.

Figure 21. Marisco Tavern Lundy Island. *Photographed by Christopher D. Thompson*

The Marisco team's first task was to create a Marisco Vineyard identity. With the medieval nature of the ancestors, the logo was developed to reflect a traditional wax seal. The type form in the seal combines both the 'M' of Marisco and 'V' of Vineyards.

Of the many discovered stories regarding the de Marisco history, a select few were chosen for their intrigue, and the essence of each was then distilled down to a single word. This was then matched with the characteristics of a particular grape variety, thus becoming the King's Bastard Chardonnay, the King's Favour Sauvignon Blanc, the King's Thorn Pinot Gris, the King's Wrath Pinot Noir, and A Sticky End Noble Sauvignon Blanc.

Brent wanted to capture the interest and imagination of the viewers while they are perusing a wine list or viewing the bottles in-store. (Figure 22)

Figure 22. The Kings Series wine from Marisco Vineyards

Brent Marris is a true entrepreneur and, like his ancestors, every bit as ambitious. He entertains buyers from all over the world at his beautiful vineyard in the Marlborough region. He has an intriguing River Hut on the banks of the Waihopai River and offers all manner of entertainment for his guests: clay bird shooting, extreme golf, and archery. He also offers game shooting on his and Rosemary's newly-purchased 5,000-acre sheep and cattle station, 'Leefield'. This is situated only 4 km from their winery.

To fulfil his business and promotional meetings, Brent flies to all parts of the world promoting the sales of his wines. The end result: stunning wines, appealing presentation, fascinating stories behind each variety—all because of the notorious Marisco background which has brought history and present day together. Thus, once again the Marisco name has awoken and will live on in many people's hearts.

These days, the Marris family have achieved acclaim for their success in the pursuit of making fine wines, with the next generation already stepping up to carry on their family's dream. Brent and Rosemary's eldest daughter, Emma, has just completed her winemaking degree at the same university Brent went to thirty years ago. The three-generation photo (Figure 23) shows Brent Marris, daughter Emma and Brent's father John Marris.

Wines from the Marisco Vineyards Waihopai Valley property have now won more than 55 gold medals and seven trophies over the past three years.

The final word, fittingly, comes from Brent Marris:

"We hereby honour our glorious family history by naming a series of wines, 'The Kings Series', after stories of our scandalous ancestors."

Figure 23. Three generations: Brent, left, Emma and John Marris

About the Author

Margaret Nyhon lives in Alexandra, in the Central Otago province of New Zealand, where she writes, paints and practises the crafts of printing and bookbinding. She has worked extensively in hospitality management in New Zealand and resort management in Australia.

The urge to trace her family history led Margaret to her most recent venture, the writing of her first non-fiction work, *de Marisco*. Margaret is married and has three adult children and two grandsons.

You can contact Margaret at margaretf@hotmail.co.nz.

www.ingramcontent.com/pod-product-compliance
Lightning Source LLC
Chambersburg PA
CBHW041259040426
42334CB00028BA/3084